Sacar, Keeper of Glory
Volume I

Adam's Covering
Volume II

by
REV. T. WHITE

TRAFFORD

Canada • UK • Ireland • USA • Spain

Note for Librarians: a cataloguing record for this book that
includes Dewey Decimal Classification and US Library of
Congress numbers is available from the National Library of
Canada. The complete cataloguing record can be obtained
from the National Library's online database at:
www.nlc-bnc.ca/amicus/index-e.html
ISBN 1-4120-3312-8
Printed in Victoria, BC, Canada

TRAFFORD

Offices in Canada, USA, Ireland, UK and Spain
This book was published *on-demand* in cooperation with
Trafford Publishing. On-demand publishing is a unique
process and service of making a book available for retail sale
to the public taking advantage of on-demand
manufacturing and Internet marketing. On-demand
publishing includes promotions, retail sales, manufacturing,
order fulfilment, accounting and collecting
royalties on behalf of the author.
Books sales in Europe:
Trafford Publishing (UK) Ltd., Enterprise House, Wistaston
Road Business Centre, Wistaston Road, Crewe CW2 7RP
UNITED KINGDOM
phone 01270 251 396 (local rate 0845 230 9601)
facsimile 01270 254 983; info.uk@trafford.com
Book sales for North America and international:
Trafford Publishing, 6E–2333 Government St.,
Victoria, BC V8T 4P4 CANADA
phone 250 383 6864 (toll-free 1 888 232 4444)
fax 250 383 6804; email to bookstore@trafford.com

www.trafford.com/robots/04-1139.html

10 9 8 7 6 5 4 3 2 1

For additional copies of this publication, contact:

Tony White, Pastor
New Life Christian Ministries
of Central Texas
702 N. 8th street
Killeen, TX 76541

Phone: 254-618-5223
E-mail: tacwhitefamily@aol.com

1. All Scripture quotations in these books were taken from the King James Version of the Bible.
2. All Hebrew and Greek definitions were taken from Biblesoft's New Exhaustive Strong's Numbers and Concordance with Expanded Greek-Hebrew Dictionary. Copyright © 1994 Biblesoft and International Bible Translators, Inc.
3. All definitions of English words were taken from the Merriam-Webster's Collegiate Dictionary, Tenth Edition.

VOLUME I

SACAR,
KEEPER OF GLORY!

Special Thanks:

First of all, I offer thanks to Jesus Christ who
inspired this work and all those who had a helping
hand in putting it together:
Abby White, Christina Nunemaker-White,
Kelley Nunemaker, Evangelist R. Simmons and
Delores Bellinger.

INTRODUCTION

Why does God's Word command a lifestyle different then that of the world? Why does His Spirit lead us in ways not understood by others? Why does His Word bring conviction to my heart about the things I am doing and those things I should be doing?

How do I let my light shine? Is my life pleasing before the Lord? How important is it to come out of the world and be separate? How is this accomplished? What kind of authority and power do I have? How do I walk in the victory I already have in Christ? Can I bring honor and glory to Jesus, my King?

Questions; all of us have so many questions. I am praying some of these inquiries will be answered in this book. Please read it with an open heart. Lean not to the understanding of the world. I believe you will be enlightened to why fellow believers do the things we do and live the way we live.

God loves you so very much. He has given you a gift more valuable than anything or anyone on earth. In this book, I will endeavor to allow the Lord to move through me to show you what that gift is, how to keep it, and how to protect it.

I invite you to take this journey with me. Take a look at what God has revealed. I trust that with each step of the way your thinking and your living will be transformed. Each page will bring a better and clearer understanding of the questions you have.

Answers, real answers, can only come from God. He uses tools and vessels made of clay. You and I are those vessels. God desires to use you in very unique ways.

Let us begin this expedition while trusting God along the path. Demonstrate faith by believing, hoping, and experiencing the power of mysteries solved in His holy word.

CHAPTER I

SACAR!

This pilgrimage begins in a small country home in the community of Kempner, Texas. I was trying to sleep. There is nothing like a good night of rest. Yet, the Lord had other ideas. Have you been there? I was covered with blankets and sleeping so peacefully when suddenly something woke me. Even when it is God, so many times we resist getting up and praying. We just want to lie there and pray, "God do I really have to get up? I can pray right here under the covers." I have tried this type of praying. It puts me right back to sleep. In fact, if you are having trouble sleeping try praying in bed. You will be lulled back to sleep.

This night the Lord spoke to my heart the word "Sacar". I could not get "Sacar" out of my mind. The word seemed to pull me out of slumber and into the living room to commune with God. Is there such a word? Is it in the Bible? What does it mean? God spoke to my heart much as my earthly father would have when I was a young child. He simply said, "Look it up." "But Lord, can you just tell me what it means?" It seems we mortals are always looking for a way without effort, discipline or sweat. I repented and reached for the *Strong's Concordance*. Thus, this journey began.

I found the word Sacar located in the Bible in two places, I Chronicles 11:35 and I Chronicles 26:4.

"Ahiam the son of Sacar the Hararite, Eliphal the son of Ur" (I Chronicles 11:35).

"Moreover the sons of Obed-edom were, Shemaiah the firstborn, Jehozabad the second, Joah the third, and Sacar the fourth, and Nethaneel the fifth" (I Chronicles 26:4).

Lord, what are you trying to show me? In which of these verses can I find the answer? And by the way, what does Sacar mean? Again He spoke to my heart. You guessed it, "Look it up." So I settled on the second reference location, I Chronicles 26:4, and began to look at Sacar according to the Hebrew meaning.

Sacar means *recompense*. It was taken from a word meaning *compensation*, *payment* or *wages*. The Lord really had my attention now. What kind of recompense and what kind of compensation? Was it a spiritual wage or a worldly wage? Who was this Sacar? Why was the Lord speaking to me about him? He was the fourth son of Obed-edom. Who was Obed-edom?

Was he the Obed-edom whose house was blessed because the Ark of the Covenant was lodged in his home for three months? Is he the Obed-edom that was the doorkeeper of the Ark? I believe he was the one and the same. "And the ark of God remained with the family of Obed-edom in his house three months. And the LORD blessed the house of Obed-edom, and all that he had" (I Chronicles 13:14).

"And Shebaniah, and Jehoshaphat, and Nethaneel,

and Amasai, and Zechariah, and Benaiah, and Eliezer, the priests, did blow with the trumpets before the ark of God: and Obed-edom and Jehiah were doorkeepers for the ark.

So David, and the elders of Israel, and the captains over thousands, went to bring up the ark of the covenant of the LORD out of the house of Obed-edom with joy" (I Chronicles 15:24-25).

I was becoming enthralled. "Lord can we get there already?" God spoke to my soul, "Patience."

I remember back to a time as a child I was eating pecans. My babysitter was cracking them and pulling away the shell so I could eat. I was throwing a small fit wanting the pecan immediately. So, he gave it to me. I popped it in my mouth and began to chew. It was not long before I spit it out because the taste was so bitter. He laughed at my mishap. I wanted the pecan so much and could not wait until he had time to shell the pecan thoroughly. Part of the shell was still between the fruit of the pecan. We tend to be like this with spiritual things. God wants us to wait until the fruit is completely shelled and all that remains is the good taste of the Word. I closed my mouth and waited on God. Oh, to wait upon the Lord! It is always worth the wait!

Sacar was a Porter in the House of God.

"Concerning the divisions of the porters: Of the Korhites was Meshelemiah the son of Kore, of the sons of Asaph" (I Chronicles 26:1).

"Moreover the sons of Obed-edom were, Shemaiah the firstborn, Jehozabad the second, Joah the third, and

Sacar the fourth, and Nethaneel the fifth" (1 Chronicles 26:4).

Lord, what does Porter mean? Right…. I went to look it up. Porter in the Hebrew language means a *janitor, a doorkeeper*. I was thinking, "Is this my compensation to be a janitor or a doorkeeper?" Wait a minute. David said, "For a day in thy courts is better than a thousand. I had rather be a doorkeeper in the house of my God, than to dwell in the tents of wickedness" (Psalms 84:10).

Maybe there is something more to being a porter, janitor or a doorkeeper than I realize.

Porter was taken from a word meaning a *gatekeeper*. "Lord, are you trying to tell me I am a guard to a door? This is my recompense, my compensation, and my wage?"

"Yes," He answered to my heart. "Lord, you woke me up to tell me I am a Sacar, a porter, a janitor, a doorkeeper or gatekeeper.

"Yes," He spoke to my soul. "Please Lord, may we get to the point?" Right…. I closed my mouth and listened.

I was hungry to know what God was trying to show me. I looked up the word doorkeeper in the Hebrew language. It means to *snatch away, to terminate and to wait at the threshold*.

Suddenly two verses of scripture flooded my mind. "Behold, I stand at the door, and knock: if any man hear my voice, and open the door, I will come in to him, and will sup with him, and he with me. To him that overcometh will I grant to sit with me in my throne, even as I also overcame, and am set down with my Father in his throne" (Revelation 3:20-21).

"And I will give unto thee the keys of the kingdom of heaven: and whatsoever thou shalt bind on earth shall be bound in heaven: and whatsoever thou shalt loose on earth shall be loosed in heaven" (Matthew 16:19).

Amazing! Sacar, a porter, has the keys to open or shut the door, the authority to keep out or allow in. I was jolted wide wake. Lead on, Lord.

Where did these porters come from? How did it all start? What are their duties?

The Lord spoke to my heart to go to sleep. But Lord, I am not sleepy. Right.... I went back to bed.

CHAPTER II

CHOSEN BY GOD!

About two years passed before the Lord impressed upon me to continue this journey. Where was I supposed to begin? Let us start with Moses and the deliverance of God's people out of Egypt. Egypt is a type of sin. "For all have sinned, and come short of the glory of God" (Romans 3:23).

Spiritually, all mankind have lived in Egypt. All have come short of the glory of God. The quest began. "What are you telling me, Lord?" He reminded me of patience. I had learned the valuable lesson. I closed my mouth again and waited.

God led them with a pillar of cloud by day and a pillar of by fire by night. God used Moses to lead His people out of Egypt. They found themselves at the Red Sea. We have all been there before. It is a place in life that felt impossible to cross. The situation you came from appears better than where you are headed. As you look back you see the enemy waiting to devour you just as Israel did. Yet God Almighty parted the Red Sea and Moses led them safely to the other side. Their enemy was destroyed as the waters returned.

Afterwards, God led Moses to Mount Sinai. Moses

went to the top of the mountain for forty days. He did not eat anything.

At this point I wondered if God would ask me not to eat anything for forty days. Whew, He did not.

While Moses was gone, things went sour to say the least. God gave Moses His commandments on how the Israelites were to live. He also gave them the design of the tabernacle where God would dwell and speak to His people.

The tabernacle consisted of three basic parts: the outer court wherein the brazen altar and the brazen laver were; the inner court wherein was the golden table of shewbread; golden altar, and the golden candlestick were; and the Holy of Holies wherein was the Ark of the Covenant. Inside the Ark was Aaron's rod that budded, a pot of manna, and the two tables of stone also known as the Ten Commandments.

What about the Israelites? What were they up to while Moses was gone? Something was happening. People were bringing their earrings and bracelets and giving them to Moses' brother Aaron.

Aaron was making something. It was a golden calf. The people of Israel began to worship this image and said this was their god who brought them out of Egypt.

God's anger waxed hot. You know about anger don't you. It is hot! God said the people had become stiff-necked and He was going to destroy them.

I looked for the Porters but I could not find them. I wondered what this had to do with them. God spoke, "Be patient." I have a very hard time with patience, do you? I closed my mouth and listened.

Moses interceded for the people and God repented or changed His mind. Praise God. At times He will change His mind; but never His principles.

When Moses saw how the people had sinned he threw down the tables of stone breaking them. He saw the people were naked. You see, nakedness and evil will always be the result of wickedness entering into the heart of man. Moses cried, "Who is on the Lord's side?" Listen. Can you hear the sound? Who is on the Lord's side? Who will follow Him?

"And he said to them all, If any man will come after me, let him deny himself, and take up his cross daily, and follow me. For whosoever will save his life shall lose it: but whosoever will lose his life for my sake, the same shall save it" (Luke 9:23-24).

"Jesus," I cried, "I want to be on your side. Show me the way. Teach me your words. Let me walk in your paths." I was a little concerned. "Jesus, are you trying to tell me I have allowed wickedness to enter my heart?"

Again Jesus spoke to me, "Sacar, keepers of the glory." They are porters, janitors, doorkeepers in the house of God. God has given them the keys and the authority. Lord, I do not get it. Please take my hand and lead me through. You have been there. You may be there now. Reach out and take His hand and follow Him.

The tribe of Levi was the only one to gather around

Moses in support and obedience. Levi was the grand-father to Aaron and Moses.

"And these are the names of the sons of Levi according to their generations; Gershon, and Kohath, and Merari: and the years of the life of Levi were an hundred thirty and seven years. The sons of Gershon; Libni, and Shimi, according to their families.

And the sons of Kohath; Amram, and Izhar, and Hebron, and Uzziel: and the years of the life of Kohath were an hundred thirty and three years.

And the sons of Merari; Mahali and Mushi: these are the families of Levi according to their generations" (Exodus 6:16-19).

"I don't understand, Lord." Right........I looked it up. The Porters were chosen from the tribe of Levi.

"And the LORD spake unto Moses, saying, And I, behold, I have taken the Levites from among the children of Israel instead of all the firstborn that openeth the matrix among the children of Israel: therefore the Levites shall be mine;" (Numbers 3:11-12).

God chose them the way He chooses us today. I have been places where no one wanted me on their side. I stood alone wanting to hear my name called. I listened but the call never came. Yet with God all things are possible. You know what I am talking about. Listen to the call of the gospel. You are a chosen generation. God has called you out of your particular darkness into newness of life.

"But ye are a chosen generation, a royal priesthood, an holy nation, a peculiar people; that ye should shew forth the praises of him who hath called you out of darkness into his marvellous light: Which in time past were not a people, but are now the people of God: which had not obtained mercy, but now have obtained mercy" (I Peter 2:9-10).

The Levites were chosen to be Porters. Sacar was a Porter. What a honor; Sacar, keepers of the glory.

"Concerning the divisions of the porters: Of the Korhites was Meshelemiah the son of Kore, of the sons of Asaph, And the sons of Meshelemiah were, Zechariah the firstborn, Jediael the second, Zebadiah the third, Jathniel the fourth, Elam the fifth, Jehohanan the sixth, Elioenai the seventh. Moreover the sons of Obed-edom were, Shemaiah the firstborn, Jehozabad the second, Joah the third, and Sacar the fourth, and Nethaneel the fifth" (I Chronicles 26:1-4).

The Levites were chosen at Mount Sinai, when they gathered around Moses to be on the Lord's side. They had not worshiped the golden calf. They had not allowed wickedness to enter their hearts; therefore they became the doorkeepers of the house of God. The tabernacle was a place where the glory of God dwelt and communed with them.

What were their duties and their purpose? I wanted to know; but God would not reveal it to me until I looked it up. "Lord, would not it be much easier to give me a vision or a dream instead of all this studying." There was no answer. I already knew the answer. The journey can be difficult and lengthy. But, oh the joy of things learned along the way!

CHAPTER III

REASONABLE SERVICE!

Service, reasonable service, what does that mean to you? I believe scripture gives us a perfect definition.

"I beseech you therefore, brethren, by the mercies of God, that ye present your bodies a living sacrifice, holy, acceptable unto God, which is your reasonable service. And be not conformed to this world: but be ye transformed by the renewing of your mind, that ye may prove what is that good, and acceptable, and perfect, will of God" (Romans 12:1-2).

Sacrifice, wait a minute, means *death*. Sacrifice, is giving up something valuable. There is a cost involved. "Lord, am I hearing you correctly?" Right..... I closed my mouth and continued to read in I Chronicles chapter 9.

I found the service of porters to be more than just guarding a door. As well as being keepers of the gates of the tabernacle, their service included work within. They were responsible for the instruments of the sanctuary, the flour, oil, wine, frankincense and the spices. They had charge of the ministering vessels, bringing them in and out by count. They lodged around the house of God and opened the doors every morning.

They were entrusted with the chambers and treasuries of the Lord's holy temple. They made showbread every Sabbath.

This sounds labor intensive. This was a great responsibility since the tabernacle is where God dwelt and spoke to Israel.

In Chronicles 15:23 I found they were even doorkeepers for the Ark of the Covenant. In II Chronicles 23:19 they were not to let anything unclean enter into the tabernacle.

The porters were to insure the tabernacle remained holy and pure. The things of God were kept sanctified and fit for the Master's use. My mind and heart were racing with so many thoughts. What about you? What are you feeling or thinking? Think about their reasonable service to stand and watch for things that would defile the temple. They had the authority to repel any type of wickedness that would try and enter this consecrated place.

This sounds like an around the clock job minus vacation or sleep. Lord, I am excited but also a little concerned. Are you trying to tell me to never take a vacation or sleep? Silence… nothing but silence. Scriptures began to come to my heart.

"But ye, brethren, are not in darkness, that that day should overtake you as a thief. Ye are all the children of light, and the children of the day: we are not of the night, nor of darkness. Therefore let us not sleep, as do others; but let us watch and be sober. For they that sleep, sleep in the night; and they that be drunken are drunken in the night. But let us, who are of the day, be sober, putting on the breastplate of faith and love; and for a helmet, the hope of salvation," (I Thessalonians 5:4-8).

"Be sober, be vigilant; because your adversary the devil, as a roaring lion, walketh about, seeking whom he may devour:" (I Peter 5:8).

I said, "I see, Lord. I must spiritually stay alert and watch." I could see a soldier on guard duty asking, "Who goes there?" Porters were the same way. They said, "Who goes there?" But, they were not listening for a password. They were looking for whether something was clean or unclean, righteous or wicked. They stood ready to open the door or keep it shut. They understood their service unto the Lord and their responsibility to maintain the tabernacle in the right condition.

I was beginning to feel better about being a Sacar, a porter, a janitor or doorkeeper in the house of God. I was gaining understanding about the compensation and wages that come with this calling. What an honor and privilege to stand at the door of the temple watching and guarding the glory of God.

Indeed Sacar was a keeper of the glory. What is glory and how can a porter affect it? It seemed as though I never ran out of questions. What about you? I wanted to know and I wanted to understand.

In Old Testament Hebrew, glory means *splendor* or *copiousness* (ko-pe-es-ness) {yielding something abundant like a harvest or springs} taken from a word meaning *chargeable*. Porters were chargeable in their service to insure nothing would be allowed in that would corrupt the splendor and copiousness of God's glory. They were allowed the greatest honor on this earth.

Glory, in the New Testament Greek, means *dignity*, *honor*, *praise* and *worship*. It was taken from a word meaning *accounted* and *reputation*.

Porters must stay alert for their service could bring reproach upon the dignity and honor of God's glory by allowing unclean things to enter into the tabernacle. They were charged and accountable for the reputation of the tabernacle by their service at the entry points into the place where God dwelt.

Some of the pieces of the puzzle were beginning to come together; but the picture was still a little fuzzy.

How can a Porter affect the glory of God within the tabernacle? How can his service bring reproach upon the honor and dignity of God's tabernacle? Can God's glory lift from the tabernacle and if so has this happened? How important is God's glory to me? Where does God's glory actually dwell in the tabernacle? I am not even going to ask you Lord; but I am just going to go and look it up. Right......

CHAPTER IV

GLORY!

The tabernacle was God's dwelling place. To review, the tabernacle consisted of three basic parts, the outer court, the inner court and the Holy of Holies. God chose to dwell in the Holy of Holies between the two cherubims above the mercy seat.

"And the cherubims shall stretch forth their wings on high, covering the mercy seat with their wings, and their faces shall look one to another; toward the mercy seat shall the faces of the cherubims be. And thou shalt put the mercy seat above upon the ark; and in the ark thou shalt put the testimony that I shall give thee. And there I will meet with thee, and I will commune with thee from above the mercy seat, from between the two cherubims which are upon the ark of the testimony, of all things which I will give thee in commandment unto the children of Israel" (Exodus 25:20-22).

"And when Moses was gone into the tabernacle of the congregation to speak with him, then he heard the voice of one speaking unto him from off the mercy seat that was upon the ark of testimony, from between the two cherubims: and he spake unto him" (Numbers 7:89).

Other scriptures regarding further evidence of God's

dwelling place above the mercy seat and between the two cherubims are found in: II Samuel 6:2, II Kings 19:15, and Isaiah 37:16.

Along with the presence of God was fire. God is a consuming fire.

"Then I looked, and, behold, in the firmament that was above the head of the cherubims there appeared over them as it were a sapphire stone, as the appearance of the likeness of a throne. And he spake unto the man clothed with linen, and said, Go in between the wheels, even under the cherub, and fill thine hand with coals of fire from between the cherubims, and scatter them over the city. And he went in in my sight" (Ezekiel 10:1-2).

"And the cherubims lifted up their wings, and mounted up from the earth in my sight: when they went out, the wheels also were beside them, and every one stood at the door of the east gate of the LORD's house; and the glory of the God of Israel was over them above" (Ezekiel 10:19).

There were also other creatures created by God to worship and praise Him day and night. They are called seraphims. They cried "Holy, holy, holy is the Lord of hosts."

"In the year that king Uzziah died I saw also the Lord sitting upon a throne, high and lifted up, and his train filled the temple.

Above it stood the seraphims: each one had six wings; with twain he covered his face, and with twain he covered his feet, and with twain he did fly. And one cried unto another, and said, Holy, holy, holy, is the LORD of hosts: the whole earth is full of his glory. And the posts of the door moved at the voice of him that cried, and the house was filled with smoke. Then said I, Woe is me! For I am undone; because I am a man of unclean lips, and I dwell in the midst of a people of unclean lips: for mine eyes have seen the King, the LORD of hosts. Then flew one of the seraphims unto me, having a live coal in his hand, which he had taken with the tongs from off the altar: And he laid it upon my mouth, and said, Lo, this hath touched thy lips; and thine iniquity is taken away, and thy sin purged" (Isaiah 6:1-7).

"And the four beasts had each of them six wings about him; and they were full of eyes within: and they rest not day and night, saying, Holy, holy, holy, Lord God Almighty, which was, and is, and is to come" (Revelation 4:8).

Between the cherubims and the seraphims and above the mercy seat was the Spirit of God and fire. This chapter has many scriptures. It is the only way to gain true understanding of the mysteries or hidden truths within the Bible. Hang on! Finish this course! The best is yet to come!

Porters were not just standing watch for a literal building; but for the very presence of God and His glory.

There within the Holy of Holies dwelt the presence of the Lord. Imagine a porter, a janitor, a doorkeeper was entrusted with the protection of this dwelling place; a place where the Shekinah Glory of God dwelt and spoke to the people of Israel to lead and teach them His ways. God chose them and gave them the keys and authority to His house. What recompense! The riches of His compensation were poured out upon their lives. All this because of the day the tribe of Levi decided to be on the Lord's side.

"Lord," I cried, "I want this compensation, this wage and service to your house. I want to stand guard and watch to insure your dignity is not compromised." I could feel my heart pounding so hard and fast I could hardly control myself. I felt like shouting or weeping or doing something to let God know I wanted to be a Sacar, keeper of the glory! How are you feeling? What are you experiencing? Do you still have questions? I do too. Let us go and find the answers!

In Hebrews, chapter 8, the Old Testament is a shadow of the New Testament. Under the New Testament, our body spiritually represents the temple of the Holy Ghost. I could hardly keep together all the scriptures flooding my soul.

"I indeed baptize you with water unto repentance: but he that cometh after me is mightier than I, whose shoes I am not worthy to bear: he shall baptize you with the Holy Ghost, and with fire: Whose fan is in his hand, and he will throughly purge his floor, and gather his wheat into the garner; but he will burn up the chaff with unquenchable fire" (Matthew 3:11-12).

"And when the day of Pentecost was fully come, they were all with one accord in one place. And suddenly there came a sound from heaven as of a rushing mighty wind, and it filled all the house where they were sitting. And there appeared unto them cloven tongues like as of fire, and it sat upon each of them. And they were all filled with the Holy Ghost, and began to speak with other tongues, as the Spirit gave them utterance" (Acts 2:1-4).

I was shouting and weeping at the same time. Praise God for His glory now dwells in the heart of men or the spiritual Holy of Holies. When His glory comes into my heart through the baptism of the Holy Ghost and fire, I become a Porter, keeper of the glory. I am *chargeable*, *accountable* to watch and be sure nothing unclean enters into the temple. God gives me the keys and authority to bind and loose, to open and shut the doors entering into the temple of God, my physical body.

I am now in charge of the temple and the spiritual instruments within. These include, the brazen altar of repentance, the brazen laver of baptism, the golden altar of praise, the golden candlestick allowing the light of God's glory to shine through my life. The table of shewbread which is the Word of God, the Ark of the Covenant, wherein lies the mercy seat to which the blood of Christ was applied. Now it is not between cherubims or seraphims but within my heart dwells the very presence of God's Spirit and His glory!

"What? Know ye not that your body is the temple of the Holy Ghost which is in you, which ye have of God, and ye are not your own? For ye are bought with a price: therefore glorify God in your body, and in your spirit, which are God's" (I Corinthians 6:19-20).

"And what agreement hath the temple of God with idols? For ye are the temple of the living God; as God hath said, I will dwell in them, and walk in them; and I will be their God, and they shall be my people. Wherefore come out from among them, and be ye separate, saith the Lord, and touch not the unclean thing; and I will receive you" (II Corinthians 6:16-17).

"Know ye not that ye are the temple of God, and that the Spirit of God dwelleth in you? If any man defile the temple of God, him shall God destroy; for the temple of God is holy, which temple ye are" (I Corinthians 3:16-17).

God has sanctified us and set us apart for very important service. We are to be porters, janitors and doorkeepers to the house of God thus not allowing anything unclean to enter into His temple. We are to keep and protect His glory from corruptible things, maintaining the splendor, the copiousness, the dignity, the honor and the reputation. We are also to shew forth praises of Him that called us out of darkness into His marvelous light or glory.

Once a person is truly born again they become the temple of God's spirit and glory. God's glory fills us, sanctifies us, and crowns us with a diadem of beauty. We have three basic parts, the outer court, the inner court and the Holy of Holies. I will expound on this in the chapter entitled "Doors."

"Then a cloud covered the tent of the congregation, and the glory of the LORD filled the tabernacle" (Exodus 40:34).

"And there I will meet with the children of Israel, and the tabernacle shall be sanctified by my glory" (Exodus 29:43).

"In that day shall the LORD of hosts be for a crown of glory, and for a diadem of beauty, unto the residue of his people, And for a spirit of judgment to him that sitteth in judgment, and for strength to them that turn the battle to the gate" (Isaiah 28:5-6).

This crown of glory is given to those that battle at the gate or door. No wonder Paul says to fight the good fight of faith, enduring to the end!

"I have fought a good fight, I have finished my course, I have kept the faith: Henceforth there is laid up for me a crown of righteousness, which the Lord, the righteous judge, shall give me at that day: and not to me only, but unto all them also that love his appearing" (II Timothy 4:7-8).

"And every man that striveth for the mastery is temperate in all things. Now they do it to obtain a corruptible crown; but we an incorruptible. I therefore so run, not as uncertainly; so fight I, not as one that beateth the air: But I keep under my body, and bring it into subjection: lest that by any means, when I have preached to others, I myself should be a castaway" (I Corinthians 9:25-27).

What happens when unclean things enter into the temple? How does this happen? How can it be prevented? Questions, I have so many questions.

CHAPTER V

ICHABOD

Have you ever felt distant from the Lord? You have been there and so have I. Why? There are, I am sure, many reasons. Could one reason be that the glory of God has lifted from my life and from my heart? Could one reason be I have allowed unclean things to enter into my heart causing the glory of God to be removed? Is that why I feel powerless? Is that why it is hard to pray and worship God? Is the spiritual splendor missing? Are you not on fire for the Lord like you once were?

This chapter will cover Ichabod; the glory is departed from Israel. The chapters following will show us how the corrupt and unclean things enter into our heart, the temple of the Holy Ghost, and what we can do to prevent it. Do not be discouraged but rather rejoice; the best is yet to come!

I want to look at two examples in scripture. The first deals with Eli, his sons, and Samuel. The second example deals with Israel.

Eli was the High Priest of Israel and had two sons who served Belial and knew not the Lord. They were doing things that were evil. They even sinned inside the tabernacle. Wickedness must have entered into their hearts. Eli tried to stop them but they continued to transgress the commandments of the Lord. The Lord spoke to Samuel that both Eli's sons would die for a sign. Then something very dreadful took place. The lamp of God, where the Ark was, went out. The glory of God had departed.

Where were the Porters? What were they doing? Were they sleeping on the job? Were they closing their eyes to sin? Remember they had the charge of and were accountable to the house of God.

"And their charge shall be the ark, and the table, and the candlestick, and the altars, and the vessels of the sanctuary wherewith they minister, and the hanging, and all the service thereof" (Numbers 3:31).

The next morning Samuel opened the doors to the temple, not the Porters. Samuel feared to tell Eli the vision God gave him. Eli pressed him until Samuel told him all. Eli knew it was from God yet failed to do anything about it.

Many times in my life, and maybe yours, we know things are not right but fail to do something about it. Possibly this is because we do not know what to do or how to do it. Has the lamp of God gone out in your heart? Are you wondering if it matters how we live or act? Please hold on. Stay with me and I believe God will help you to relight the lamp.

The Ark was taken by the Philistines. Eli's two sons were killed in battle. Eli fell off his seat and broke his neck and died. Eli's daughter-in-law died during child birth and named her son Ichabod, meaning *the glory of God is departed from Israel.*

All of this took place because things unclean were allowed to enter into the temple. The porters must have become complacent in their duties. They must have taken bribes from the world. They forgot whose side they were on. They must have thought God's glory would never depart from Israel.

The second example is from Ezekiel chapter 11. God took Ezekiel to the east gate of the Lord's house. At the door of the gate there were twenty-five men. These men devised mischief and gave wicked counsel to the city. At the door to the Lord's house men were planning evil against the city. The glory of God departed from the city and went to the mountain east of it.

"Then did the cherubims lift up their wings, and the wheels beside them; and the glory of the God of Israel was over them above. And the glory of the LORD went up from the midst of the city, and stood upon the mountain which is on the east side of the city" (Ezekiel 11:22-23).

It is the same old tool to sow evil and wickedness in the heart of man, to go through the gates into the outer court and then into the inner court until it has entered in the heart of man. Our enemy's whole purpose is to destroy us and corrupt the splendor of God in our lives.

Oh, God do not leave me here. There must be an answer. There must be a way to keep unclean things out of the temple. Do not close the book now. We are so close to the answer. Remember, He gave us the power, authority and the keys to the Kingdom of Heaven.

"..and I will fill this house with glory, saith the Lord of hosts. The silver is mine, and the gold is mine, saith the Lord of hosts. The glory of this latter house shall be greater than of the former, saith the Lord of hosts: and in this place will I give peace, saith the Lord of hosts" (Haggai 2:7-9). We are that house not made with hands but fashioned by the very hand of God.

God removed the stony heart and replaced it with a heart of flesh, a place to write His laws and dwell with His people.

"And I will give them one heart, and I will put a new spirit within you; and I will take the stony heart out of their flesh, and will give them an heart of flesh: That they may walk in my statutes, and keep mine ordinances, and do them: and they shall be my people, and I will be their God. But as for them whose heart walketh after the heart of their detestable things and their abominations, I will recompense their way upon their own heads, saith the Lord GOD" (Ezekiel 11:19-21).

"This is the covenant that I will make with them after those days, saith the Lord, I will put my laws into their hearts, and in their minds will I write them; And their sins and iniquities will I remember no more" (Hebrews 10:16-17).

We are now the temple of the Holy Ghost and the porters of the tabernacle. Yes, we are Sacar, keeper of the glory. Many believe it does not matter how we live, act or dress because of grace. Also, many believe, God's glory will never depart His temple. However, God will not dwell in an unclean temple and will destroy those that defile it.

"And what concord hath Christ with Belial? or what part hath he that believeth with an infidel? And what agreement hath the temple of God with idols? for ye are the temple of the living God; as God hath said, I will dwell in them, and walk in them; and I will be their God, and they shall be my people. Wherefore come out from among them, and be ye separate, saith the Lord, and touch not the unclean thing; and I will receive you" (II Corinthians 6:15-17).

"Know ye not that ye are the temple of God, and that the Spirit of God dwelleth in you? If any man defile the temple of God, him shall God destroy; for the temple of God is holy, which temple ye are" (I Corinthians 3:16-17).

The command has not changed. We are to watch and close the door to the things of wickedness and uncleanness in the world. We are not responsible for making atonement for our sins because Jesus alone did that. We are, however, responsible for the doors into our mind and heart, ensuring God's glory stays pure and His splendor bright. We are to ensure the wells of springing water never stop flowing and the harvest of the fruit of His Spirit never stops producing.

We are chargeable to protect the dignity and honor of God's Spirit within our temple or bodies. That is why God commands us to come out of the world and be separate. Separation from the things of the world maintains the light of God's glory in my life. It keeps the lamp lit. Remember the ten virgins, five had the lamps ready, trimmed and shining. The other five ran out of oil and the fire within the lamps went out.

I am a porter, a janitor and doorkeeper to my soul and the house of God. I am in charge of the doors; but how many doors? Where are they located? Right..... let us find out!

CHAPTER VI

DOORS!

Doors are a means to enter and exit a structure. They are a means to keep things and people out and to allow in. Doors come in all shapes, sizes and designs. Almost all exterior doors are equipped with locks. These locks are to prevent unwanted items from coming into our homes. Many exterior doors have a peep hole to see what or who is at the door before opening.

There are at least five doors or gates to the *outer court* of our body: the eyes, the ears, the mouth, the nose and the sense of touch. There is at least one door or gate to the *inner court* of our temple, the *mind*. There is one door to the *Holy of Holies*, the *heart*.

There are three ways unclean things knock on these doors, the lust of the flesh, the lust of the eyes and the pride of life, I John 2:16.

Unclean things first must enter through the doors of the outer court to get the door of the inner court and from there into the Holy of Holies. I will expound on this in a moment.

The things we see, hear, taste, smell and touch affect our thinking. Our thoughts, if not controlled, affects our heart. Our heart affects our enitre temple.

Our Eyes

In Genesis chapter three Eve saw that the tree was good for food and that it was pleasant to the eyes. If she would not have looked upon the tree she would not have eaten of the forbidden fruit. Stay with me, we will cover her ears later.

"The light of the body is the eye and when the eye is single or focused the whole body is full of light. When the eye is evil then our body is full of darkness" (Luke 11).

"I will set no evil thing before my eyes" (Psalms 101:3).

It does matter what my eyes see. What I view on TV, videos, in books, on the internet and in the world around me. I am the doorkeeper of my eyes which are the window of my soul. I must control the things I look upon. God has chosen me and given me the power, keys and authority to control my eyes.

When I open the door of my eyes to see evil things, the door to my mind is now open. My mind brings this information to the door of my heart. Therefore the battle is on. However, when I close my eyes to evil things hence I close the door to my mind and my heart; for out of the heart proceeds things that will defile the temple.

"For out of the heart proceed evil thoughts, murders, adulteries, fornications, thefts, false witness, and blasphemies: These are the things which defile a man: but to eat with unwashen hands defileth not a man" (Matthew 15:19-20).

I must realize at all times I am a Sacar, keeper of the glory. What I do in life, where I go and how I act will affect the Glory of God within me.

The Ears

If Eve would have resisted the voice of the serpent and closed the door, she would not have looked upon the tree nor eaten of the fruit. Jesus resisted the enemy's voice by the Word of God within His heart. He would not give His ear to the adversary.

"Give ear, O my people, to my law: incline your ears to the words of my mouth" "Psalms 78:1".

"For this people's heart is waxed gross, and their ears are dull of hearing, and their eyes they have closed; lest at any time they should see with their eyes, and hear with their ears, and should understand with their heart, and should be converted, and I should heal them. But blessed are your eyes, for they see: and your ears, for they hear" (Matthew 13:15-16).

"For the time will come when they will not endure sound doctrine; but after their own lusts shall they heap to themselves teachers, having itching ears; And they shall turn away their ears from the truth, and shall be turned unto fables. But watch thou in all things, endure afflictions, do the work of an evangelist, make full proof of thy ministry" (II Timothy 4:3-5).

Let us watch, standing guard at the door of the temple of the Holy Ghost. It does make a difference what I listen to whether it be music, ungodly language, or the doctrine and lies of the world. I am chargeable and accountable to God for what I allow in. I am His porter, the protector of His glory.

Think of a conversation between brothers and sisters in the Lord. You know, you have been there; maybe you are there right now. You listen to someone in the church tell you about this event or that event. They tell you about this saint or that saint, maybe even about their Pastor. Once the ears hear, then the mind knows, and will try to enter the heart. Once the thought enters the heart the battle rages. Only the Word of God will give us peace again.

Think about it; "faith cometh by hearing and hearing the Word of God" (Romans 10:17). The Word of God must first be heard through the ears before entering the mind and then into the heart to bring forth faith.

Fear can enter into the mind by going through all five doors. Once fear creeps into the mind it will try to open the door to your heart. Thus causing a physical, emotional or spiritual reaction to what was seen, heard, touched, tasted or smelled.

Touch

Lord, I am confused about touch. How can touching anything open the door into my mind? There is tremendous power in touch.

The Lord touched many lives on the earth. His word reveals that through the laying on of hands the Holy Ghost was given. By the anointing of oil many are healed. Remember the first time you held hands with someone. You did not feel very emotional until you actually held his/her hand. Your eyes saw their hand. Your mind started thinking how you could go about holding their hand. Once you touched them, wow, the feeling touched your heart. Touch has a powerful effect on the mind and in turn the heart.

"Wherefore come out from among them, and be ye separate, saith the Lord, and touch not the unclean thing; and I will receive you" (II Corinthians 6:17).

"Wherefore if ye be dead with Christ from the rudiments of the world, why, as though living in the world, are ye subject to ordinances, (Touch not; taste not; handle not; Which all are to perish with the using;) after the commandments and doctrines of men" (Colossians 2:20-22)?

Many souls have gone back into the world because of touch. Many have felt their walk with God altered because of touching things they knew better than to touch. That is why it is so very important not to touch people suddenly and to keep your hands to yourself. Be careful even to the point of hugging only those of your family or of the same gender within the church.

What door could you open by hugging another person's spouse or the opposite gender? You think this might be silly but many have fallen prey from what they thought to be an innocent hug or touch.

I want to live in such a way that my life guards the glory of God within my heart, keeping the splendor ever so bright and the honor of God ever so strong. I want to become a Sacar, keeper of glory, to be able to hear the voice of God clearly and minister to Him properly.

Taste

Here is another door I am not so sure about – tasting. Can this sense open a door to the mind and then to the heart corrupting the glory of God within my life? There are many different kinds of taste for example food, drink, righteousness, and even sin.

As a young man I can remember going out to the garden and picking cucumbers to eat with vinegar. My mouth is watering now and I can almost taste them even though there is none in my mouth. Has this ever happened with you concerning a particular food, drink or other items?

There is a spiritual taste bud as well. Doing something good or right leaves a good taste in your mouth but doing something wrong or bad leaves a bad taste.

"Return, I pray you, let it not be iniquity; yea, return again, my righteousness is in it. Is there iniquity in my tongue? cannot my taste discern perverse things" (Job 6:29-30)?

"O taste and see that the LORD is good: blessed is the man that trusteth in him" (Psalms 34:8).

"How sweet are thy words unto my taste! yea, sweeter than honey to my mouth" (Psalms 119:103)!

"(Touch not; taste not; handle not; Which all are to perish with the using;) after the commandments and doctrines of men" (Colossians 2:21-22)?

Smell

How in the world could smell open up a door to my mind? Come and see.

I found the things we do can either become a stench or sweet odor unto God. Our sacrifices will either be acceptable or rejected because of the odor they produce.

Smell can be very powerful. A garbage can, a diaper pail, and rotten food are just a few examples of stench. A rose, food cooking on the grill, and perfume are just a few examples of a sweet odor.

People trying to quit certain habits can give in to them because of smell. People trying to avoid certain lifestyles can be hindered because of smell. Smell can even damage the body because of second-hand smoke or chemicals in the air.

Smell can be a door to the mind and then to the heart, taking away from the glory of God and harming my walk with Him.

"But I have all, and abound: I am full, having received of Epaphroditus the things which were sent from you, an odour of a sweet smell, a sacrifice acceptable, wellpleasing to God" (Philippians 4:18).

"And as for the perfume which thou shalt make, ye shall not make to yourselves according to the composition thereof: it shall be unto thee holy for the LORD. Whosoever shall make like unto that, to smell thereto, shall even be cut off from his people" (Exodus 30:37-38).

"And it shall come to pass, that instead of sweet

smell there shall be stink; and instead of a girdle a rent; and instead of well set hair baldness; and instead of a stomacher a girding of sackcloth; and burning instead of beauty" (Isaiah 3:24).

Let us remember, our life must be a living sacrifice, holy and acceptable unto God which is my reasonable service. Why? I am Sacar, keeper of the glory. I am a porter, a doorkeeper, a janitor to the house of God to ensure the temple stays clean.

How do I do this, Lord? How do I keep my mind and heart from being bombarded with unclean thoughts? Right..... here we go.... I need to look it up.

KEYS OF AUTHORITY!

God gave me the keys and authority when He chose me and brought me out of darkness. We have been chosen of God, not because of who we are or any goodness of our own but because we chose to believe and follow the truth of the Bible. The man Christ Jesus paid our debt that God's Spirit, His Glory could live in us. He has charged us and we are accountable. "Whatsoever a man soweth that will he also reap. If I sow to my flesh I will reap corruption but if to the Spirit life eternal" (Galatians 6).

"And I say also unto thee, That thou art Peter, and upon this rock I will build my church; and the gates of hell shall not prevail against it. And I will give unto thee the keys of the kingdom of heaven: and whatsoever thou shalt bind on earth shall be bound in heaven: and whatsoever thou shalt loose on earth shall be loosed" (Matthew 16:18-19).

You and I have the power, keys and authority from God to bind things from entering into the outer court, the inner court and the Holy of Holies. We also have the same instructions to loose things from these areas as well.

I can choose where I go, what I see and the things I

listen to. I can decide on what enters and what stays out. I do not have to answer the phone when it rings or open the door when I hear a knock.

I can be sure that what is on the other side is wholesome and good before saying come on in. I can stay away from places that will tempt me to open up to things that will destroy my walk with God. I can live a lifestyle that will be pleasing to God and that will not bring condemnation to my heart.

I must remember; "Now therefore, if ye will obey my voice indeed, and keep my covenant, then ye shall be a peculiar treasure unto me above all people: for all the earth is mine" (Exodus 19:5).

I am a peculiar treasure; I belong to Jesus. I am His personal property. Paul said he was the prisoner of Christ. I have been bought with a price, the price of His death on Calvary. The life I live is not mine. In Him I live, move and have my very being or existence. Too many times I seem to forget who I am, Sacar, keeper of the glory. I am, by His grace or God's opportunity, His witness in this world.

I can and must close, lock, and slam the door in the face of things that would diminish the splendor of God's glory within my heart. Through a repentive prayer I can loose unclean things in my mind and heart.

I can understand what David meant when he said, "For a day in thy courts is better than a thousand elsewhere. I had rather be a doorkeeper in the house of my God, than to dwell in the tents of wickedness." "For the LORD God is a sun and shield: the LORD will give grace and glory: no good thing will he withhold from them that walk uprightly" (Ps 84:10-11).

If I am a porter, a janitor and doorkeeper in the house of God then I will not dwell in tents of wickedness. I must guard the different doors. I must choose what enters and what stays out. I must choose how to live and how to dress based of God's Holy Word. No wonder God sets order in His Church and our lives.

So many may not understand why a woman's hair is a glory to her; protecting, guarding the glory of God within her and becoming a covering for her husband. When we adorn God's temple (our body) with the things of the world we bring reproach to His name. We take away the honor and dignity of His temple (our body) by trying to look like the world. I am not better or more holy than anyone but I have been chosen through God's grace to be a porter in the house of God (my body). I must stand watch, allowing nothing unclean to enter into the Holy of Holies (my heart).

I want His splendor to shine bright in His temple, my life. I want to hear well done my good and faithful servant. I want my heart right with Him at all times because I do not know when He is coming or death is calling. I am His temple and He has given power, keys, and authority to keep the doors shut to things that would corrupt my walk with Him. If I get to the point where the doors are always opened or unlocked then all types of bugs can enter. They will begin to eat away at the treasure God has given us in earthen vessels. I must hold the key safely and not give out the combination to anyone.

I must realize God has placed us in the position of Sacar, keeper of the glory.

If I walk uprightly then no good thing will be withheld; however, if I walk after the flesh and the things of the flesh then good things will be withheld. The splendor, the dignity, and honor will be tarnished.

Ministers, hold fast to Godly principles, preach the Word, and remain instant in season, and out. Yes, find the way of the Lord to present teaching that will be effective and productive. Compromise brings nakedness before the Lord. Aaron could have held fast but rather he gave in to the people. Moses stood in the gap upon Mount Sinai and the nation of Israel was spared. Yet when he came down from the mount, he asked his brother Aaron what have you done? Aaron, you have brought a great sin upon them. Moses made them drink the gold and called those who were on the Lord's side to come unto him.

Yes, stand in the gap, intercede for the souls of man but never turn away from Godly precepts in the Word of God. Listen not to the cries of their flesh but rather tune in to the cries of their heart.

Things get hard, things seem to go wrong but God will never leave us nor forsake us when we guard and protect His glory within our lives.

Many feel this promise was made no matter how I walk, live or act. Yes, God will always love me but He will not dwell in an unclean temple. This is why He gave us power, keys and authority over sin, our flesh and the adversary of our soul. Hear the call, renew your walk, close the door and keep unclean things from your mind and heart.

Remember we overcome through the blood of the lamb and the word of our testimony. You can start today, right now. You can make up your mind and heart to close the doors on some things in your life and begin to open the door to the voice of God.

"Behold, I stand at the door, and knock: if any man hear my voice, and open the door, I will come in to him, and will sup with him, and he with me. To him that overcometh will I grant to sit with me in my throne, even as I also overcame, and am set down with my Father in his throne. He that hath an ear, let him hear what the Spirit saith unto the churches" (Revelation 3:20-22).

We have the keys and authority over the door, to open or shut it. We can open to Him and overcome. We can hear His voice if we will just open our ears to His word.

Let us walk not in pride but in the responsibility the Lord has placed upon us. Let us live not in arrogance but in fear, reverencing the glory of God dwelling within us! Wherever we go and whatever we do, let us remember: We are Sacar, keeper of glory.

ADAM'S COVERING!

INTRODUCTION

You may be new to the faith or just visiting an Apostolic church for the first time. Prayerfully consider what this book is about. Do not allow the adversary to bring condemnation into your life. Work out your own salvation with fear and trembling.

I do not want anyone to feel, "This preacher is just picking on me." Do not allow the enemy to get into your mind and say things that are not true. I love you and God loves you. Like any good father, God wants to lead us in the way we are to walk, revealing truths as we grow.

Each of us, in the Lord, is different in our maturity level. Now that is not an excuse. Please do not use that to say, "Well I do not have to grow." God will always challenge us to mature.

This volume is about something I was not expecting to receive. It all started when I was praying about a thought "More than a Rib." A sister, in our church, had shared this title with me. I felt compelled to take this thought and study for a sermon. Initially, I was going to preach to men about the correct way to treat the lady in their life. Yet God gave me deeper things than I ever dreamed.

Many times "we" are in the way. Through praying and studying God can remove our will and insert His. I began to pray, "Lord, what is it?" I started to read scripture and all of a sudden I began to say, "There is something here. There is something here! God, you are trying to show me something." As I opened my mind and spirit, God began to lead and guide.

CHAPTER I

"And the LORD God said, it is not good that the man should be alone; I will make him an help meet for him. And out of the ground the LORD God formed every beast of the field, and every fowl of the air; and brought them unto Adam to see what he would call them: and whatsoever Adam called every living creature, that was the name thereof. And Adam gave names to all cattle, and to the fowl of the air, and to every beast of the field; but for Adam there was not found an help meet for him. And the LORD God caused a deep sleep to fall upon Adam and he slept: and he took one of his ribs, and closed up the flesh instead thereof; And the rib, which the LORD God had taken from man, made he a woman, and brought her unto the man. And Adam said, This is now bone of my bones, and flesh of my flesh: she shall be called Woman, because she was taken out of Man. Therefore shall a man leave his father and his mother, and shall cleave unto his wife: and they shall be one flesh" (Genesis 2:18-24).

The adversary naturally does not want preachers to preach; especially when God gives a fresh revelation of understanding. The enemy tries to shut the mouth of the preacher. But there will always be those who will proclaim the gospel in Jesus name!

As I had previously mentioned in the introduction, I was attempting to prepare a message about the thought, "More than a Rib". A sister from our church had this title and I had asked her permission to develop it into a sermon. I was going to say this and that. But God began to deal with me. The study was not flowing as it should have. Suddenly, as I continued to study and read, there were distinct things that riveted me.

Let me start by reminding us of God's glory. Keep this in mind as we think of Adam's isolation from other humankind in the book of Genesis. God saw that it was not good for Adam to be alone. To solve this problem God made a woman. He chose not to make her from the dust of the earth but to form her and fashion her in a way unlike Adam. He chose to make her from the very bone in Adam's side. He chose for Adam and Eve to be one flesh.

On the other hand, God's glory was covered by the wings of the cherubims, so that God would not be alone. I do not know why God chose to make the angels; but He did. God can exist without them. He can exist without you and me. Adam could have survived without Eve. But Adam needed a covering.

Be patient as we explore the word. Ask God for grace to hear His voice.

First, I want to lay the foundation of this message correctly. It is imperative for you that I do this properly. I pray you see and understand this fresh insight regarding "Adam's Covering". Remember, Adam was alone. He was uncovered and God said it is not good for Adam not to be covered.

God caused Adam to fall into a deep slumber. As he slept, God removed one of his ribs. God chose this very special way to make the first woman or help-meet for Adam. Thus he created woman to provide companionship and support for Adam.

God does not need a covering but he chose the wings of a cherubim, a type of angel, to cover His shekinah glory or His presence.

Glory in the Hebrew means *splendor*, from a word meaning to be *chargeable*. In the Greek it means *dignity, honor, to be of reputation.* Hold on; you are going to like this in a moment. God created Adam. God gave Adam charge over the earth and all therein to name. But God did not want Adam to be uncovered or alone. He made a help-meet for him. Now, that word help means to *aid*; meet means *an opposite, a counterpart or mate.* Rib was really *the rib, the bone* from Adam's body. Woman means *wife*. Hallelujah!

CHAPTER II

"Now I praise you, brethren, that ye remember me in all things, and keep the ordinances, as I delivered them to you. But I would have you know, that the _head_ of every man is Christ; and the _head_ of the woman is the man; and the head of Christ is God. Every man praying or prophesying, having his head covered, dishonoureth his _head_. But every woman that prayeth or prophesieth with her head uncovered dishonoureth her _head_: for that is even all one as if she were shaven. For if the woman be not covered, let her also be shorn: but if it be a shame for a woman to be shorn or shaven, let her be covered. For a man indeed ought not to cover his head, forasmuch as he is the image and _glory_ of God: but the woman is the _glory_ of the man. For the man is not of the woman; but the woman of the man. Neither was the man created for the woman; but the woman for the man. For this cause ought the woman to have power on her _head_ because of the _angels_. Nevertheless neither is the man without the woman, neither the woman without the man, in the Lord. For as the woman is of the man, even so is the man also by the woman; but all things of God. Judge in yourselves: is it comely that a woman pray unto God uncovered? Doth not even nature itself teach you, that, if a man have long hair, it is a shame unto him? But if a woman have long hair, it is a *glory to* her: for her hair is given her for a *covering*. But if any man seem to be contentious, we have no such custom, neither the churches of God" (I Corinthians 11:2-16).

I am going to show you some things that I have never thought about in my walk with God. It has changed the way I look at my wife. And if you let it, it will change the way you look at your wife, or women in general. And women, it ought to change the way you feel about your walk with God.

Adam's Covering? God's glory was covered by the wings of the cherubims. He wants us to comprehend something. We have got to understand this insight if we want to see the power of God working in our individual lives, our family's lives, and in the body of Christ. If we do not grasp this, the power of the Holy Ghost may be hindered from moving the way God truly desires to move.

The *head* of every man is Christ. The *head* of the woman is the man. I am not going to get chauvinistic. I am not going there; please stay with me. Think spiritually as you read about Adam's covering.

In his <u>humanity</u>, the *head* of Christ is God. In reference to I Corinthians 11 verse 4 states every man – that means me because I am a man. I can not change the fact that I am a man. I was born a man. I ought to have a desire to be a man. If I have a desire to be anything but a man it is from the adversary. God did not make me a woman, He made me a man. I did not have a choice in the matter.

So every man that prayeth or prophesieth having his head (this head is his natural head) covered, dishonoreth *his* head (this head is Christ).... not his natural head but Christ. You see, sometimes we read this so fast we do not really take a look at it. If I am praying or prophesying with my head covered, outside of God's plan, then I bring dishonor to Jesus Christ, who is my head or leader. The head of every man is Christ.

Every woman that prayeth or prophesieth with her head (this is her natural head) uncovered, dishonoreth her head (this head is the man)...not her literal head, but her husband. If my wife prays or prophesies with her head uncovered she dishonors me. This is revelational!

If I pray or prophesy with my head covered, I bring dishonor to Jesus. If my wife prays or prophesies with her head uncovered, she brings dishonor to me, her husband.

Please read and meditate on verse 7 very carefully. "For a man indeed ought not to cover his head. Forasmuch as he is the *image* and *glory* of God". The man is the image and glory of God. If I cover my head, I am bringing dishonor to God because I was created in his image and glory. I am His dignity. I am His splendor. Do you understand what I am trying to say here? Ladies, do not think you are not important. You are going to see how vitally important you really are. I want to break this down because as we read above the man is the image and glory of God.

God's glory was covered. So if man is the image and glory of God, he must have a covering also. If he does not have a covering his reputation is going to be open to the evil things the adversary will bring against him. Oh, I feel the Holy Ghost! You remember what glory means? "To be of dignity, honor, reputation, splendor."

But, in verse seven, it goes on to say that the woman is the glory of the man. My wife is my glory. She is my dignity. She is my reputation. That is how important you are, women! I have never heard this before in my life. But you see, you are my dignity. You are my very reputation. Oh hallelujah! Glory to God! You see, Adam was the splendor, dignity and honor of God. But Eve was splendor, dignity and honor of Adam!

It states in verse eight that the man is not of the woman, but the woman of the man. Verse nine says that neither was the man created for the woman, but the woman for the man. God was not created for the angels. But the angels were created for God to be his covering; to cover his glory. Therefore, women were created to be man's covering. Adam did not have a covering. God said it was not good for him to be un-covered. It is not good for you to be alone. So he made a wife to give him dignity and honor; to give him the right reputation!

Verse ten states, "for this cause" – wait a minute, "**for this cause**" she was created for a covering for the man, like the angels were created for the covering of

God's glory. "For this cause ought the woman to have power on her head." Not her natural head, but man, for the head of every man is Christ and the head of every woman is the man – because of the angels. This brings it all together. I have read commentary after commentary and I have never read this before. Some say these are good angels; some say these are evil angels. But God was talking about the covering angels. He was talking about the cherubims that cover the glory of God. This was a comparison. He was comparing the woman to the angels. He was looking at Eve and the angels and saying that she should cover her husband as the angels covered His glory. So the woman covers man!

God created angels for himself. God created my wife for me. Not to misuse her but as you will see later, to honor her, because she is my glory. She is my dignity. She is my reputation. If she allows me to become spiritually uncovered, I am in trouble.

CHAPTER III

Let us be real. When a man does something he ought not do, it usually does not bring a reproach upon the woman. Not normally. But what generally happens when a wife begins to do things she is not supposed to do? Many times people say, "What is wrong with the husband? He does not have any control." Her behavior brings a reproach upon the man. Then it brings reproach upon the whole household and her children are now open to be devoured by the adversary.

We are one body, one flesh, according to verse eleven. Take a look at the church. See what is happening. You may visualize how preachers are preaching. What type of things are some letting down? What things begin to filter in? At times, it is because women are praying and prophesying uncovered. Precious sisters, realize what an important role you have in the church.

Adam needed a covering. I need a covering. Yet, it is a shame for men to have long hair because we are not to cover ourselves. My wife is my covering. My wife is my glory, my dignity and my reputation.

But if a woman have long hair it is to her a glory. There are types of hair that do not grow at the same pace. The scripture does not mean long, as much as it means "uncut". Do not cut your covering because when you do, you open a gap over your husband and you bring shame to your head (or husband). This is truth! A woman's uncut hair is a glory *to* her. It does not say it is HER glory. It says it is a glory *to her*. For her hair is given her for a *covering.*

She is literally covering her head (or husband). Spiritually, when my wife's hair begins to grow and she does not cut it, she is covering me, every part of me and every area of me. The reputation, the anointing and the unction get stronger. God shows me things that he has never shown me before. He reveals to me the things that we are reading right now. It is because of a covering. Each is free to do what we wish to do. But I am beseeching you, dear sisters, to demonstrate even more love to your husband, your pastor, your church, and the Word, by refraining from cutting your hair.

Let me share some things with you. You may choose to believe or not. I have found this following situation is true in most cases. When a woman becomes rebellious her lifestyle changes; she begins to adorn herself unbiblically. Almost immediately, she begins to cut her hair. Her husband soon begins to have troubles. You let a man fall, and often times the woman can continue to stand. It is the truth! If a man goes spiritually lax, falls out of church, or commits adultery, most of the time, women pray harder and stand stronger. But when the female begins to uncover the husband, it affects him!

In effect, when she begins to cut her hair, she is cutting him.

Recently while attending a winter conference one of the speakers began to reference his personal convictions. All of a sudden he called for his wife to come to the platform to prove his convictions. He asked her to turn around in a circle for all to see her standard of holy living. He was proud of her. He was revealing through her, his glory, dignity, splendor and reputation.

CHAPTER IV

Now men, normally it is not us that are contentious about this subject, but we have never heard it this way. We have never heard that the woman is our glory. We have never heard she is our dignity, our honor, our reputation. That is why Paul said in verse 16, (note I am paraphrasing), men, do not get the bighead thinking you are something when you are nothing. God saw you were uncovered and alone. So he brought something to protect you. He sent something of honor - something that is priceless. Do not become contentious about how important the woman, your covering, really is.

Many times this subject is used against the women. But I ought to realize how important she is to me. I ought to recognize how valuable she is to me. Literally, spiritually, she is my covering! Glory to God!

When the relationship between man and woman is in the wrong order, the glory of man departs or is corrupted. Just as the glory of God departs when unclean things come in. Women, you are vitally important to keep the church of the living God pure and holy by the way you live, the way you dress, and by your hair. It is a covering over God's church. Praise God!

But the adversary was beautiful. Women, do not get angry, please. He was vain and women tend, as well as men at times, to be the same way. The enemy loves to lie to you that you are going to be ugly if you do not cut your hair! You are not! When the enemy brings condemnation upon you defeat him; let your hair grow! Let it grow for the glory of God and as the covering to protect your mate and family!

You begin to look at yourself in the mirror and count wrinkles. You care about the way you look and you should. But caring too much about how the world perceives you, instead of how God sees you, can bring trouble. Let us care about the inward heart, which is, in the sight of God, a great price. Which would you rather have? Would it be a husband and church that are covered and living for God. Or a worldly church that the devil does anything he wants?

When women become modest and sold out they take hold of God and forget about what the world may be saying. They do this by saying and displaying, "I am going to be what God wants me to be. I am going to cover my husband, my pastor, and my church." By showing this act of faith God begins to move more deeply in their lives. He begins to touch others. He begins to draw souls with His spirit that they might be born again. I have seen it and I have experienced it myself personally.

CHAPTER V

"Thou art the anointed cherub that covereth; and I have set thee so: thou wast upon the holy mountain of God; thou hast walked up and down in the midst of the stones of fire. Thou wast perfect in thy ways from the day that thou wast created, till iniquity was found in thee. By the multitude of thy merchandise they have filled the midst of thee with violence, and thou hast sinned: therefore I will cast thee as profane out of the mountain of God: and I will destroy thee, O covering cherub, from the midst of the stones of fire. Thine heart was lifted up because of thy beauty, thou hast corrupted thy wisdom by reason of thy brightness: I will cast thee to the ground, I will lay thee before kings, that they may behold thee. Thou hast defiled thy sanctuaries by the multitude of thine iniquities, by the iniquity of thy traffick; therefore will I bring forth a fire from the midst of thee, it shall devour thee, and I will bring thee to ashes upon the earth in the sight of all them that behold thee. All they that know thee among the people shall be astonished at thee: thou shalt be a terror, and never shalt thou be any more" (Ezekiel 28:14-19).

I am not trying to hurt anybody. I am not trying to make you do anything nor mold you into what I want you to be. I am sharing the gospel as God revealed it to me. I have never heard it this way in my life. I know someone may have received it this way themselves. This is lining up with the Word. It is in harmony. It is showing the value of the woman and why she is supposed to have uncut hair – not so much measuring how long it is – but uncut. It esteems the woman with uncut hair as holy, obedient, submissive, and living a life for God in its totality!

We can look at history and our heritage. We can browse through pictures and read about past American history. You will see women with uncut hair and most men with short hair. The adversary has moved on the heart of man throughout the ages. But, I would like to focus on the period during the '60s and '70s when American youth became hippies. This occurred because of rebellion. Men began to grow their hair long and women began to cut their hair and wear mini-skirts. No wonder our country is in trouble. We no longer have a covering over our country. What began as something esteemed as small or of no importance became the beginning of moral decay. The adversary can do whatever he wants to do to our children, to our lives, to our religion, to our doctrine. Let me tell you something. How we present ourselves is important. We must get back to the magnitude of the covering. Women, let your hair be a shield over your husband, or future husband, your pastor, and your church.

Look at Ezekiel 28, the angel referenced Lucifer. He had been an anointed cherubim that covereth until iniquity was found in him. Lucifer's heart was lifted up because of his beauty; this corrupted his wisdom by reason of his brightness. He defiled his sanctuary by the multitude of his iniquity.

When wives begin to do things that they are not to do, people are astonished. There is

nothing that affects a church more than a women who once had convictions about living a lifestyle pleasing to God walk away from these convictions. It affects the entire church. You let men do the same, and the women will pray harder and hold on longer and become more convicted about living for God. But if the man becomes uncovered something wicked will take place!

I am not going to leave you here. "Likewise, ye wives, be in subjection to your own husbands; that, if any obey not the word, they also may without the word be won by the conversation of the wives; While they behold your chaste conversation coupled with fear. Whose adorning let it not be that outward adorning of plaiting the hair, and of wearing of gold, or of putting on of apparel; But let it be the hidden man of the heart, in that which is not corruptible, even the ornament of a meek and quiet spirit, which is in the sight of God of great price. For after this manner in the old time the holy women also, who trusted in God, adorned themselves, being in subjection unto their own husbands: Even as Sara obeyed Abraham, calling him lord: whose daughters ye are, as long as ye do well, and are not afraid with any amazement. Likewise, ye husbands, dwell with them according to knowledge, giving honour unto the wife, as unto the weaker vessel, and as being heirs together of the grace of life; that your prayers be not hindered" (I Peter 3:1-7).

Ladies, please understand what God has given you the privilege to do. When you dress appropriately you bring a good reputation to your husband. You are his dignity and honor. Do not be afraid of what people are going to say to you or about you.

What does honor mean? It means, *to value, to esteem of the highest degree.* You are precious; you are your husband's glory; you are his covering. Men, if we do not treat her correctly, bad things will begin to happen, and we all lose out.

Men have no business talking down to women. They have no business treating them as inferior. Don't we understand they are our glory? They are of us; we are of them; they are our covering.

I am to treat my wife with honor so that my prayers will not be hindered. If I am not treating her biblically, I might as well not pray. I should never belittle or make fun of her. I ought to lift her up. I ought to say kind things about her. I should brag on her; she is my covering, my reputation, my glory!

Do you realize that the woman is the keeper of the home (Titus 2:5)? I Timothy 3:7 says, "Moreover he must have a good report of them which are without, lest he fall into reproach and the snare of the devil."

Husbands, treat your wives (your covering) with respect. Esteem them of the highest degree that your prayers may not be hindered.

Ladies, when you begin to hear things that you think are going to distract from your beauty, recognize it is a lie from the devil. Your dedication and steadfastness will add to your shield of honor.

Employ a prayerful and loving spirit coupled with your holy adorning to keep your husband out of danger. You want to keep him out of the snare of the adversary. Prayerfully beseech God to keep him away from temptations that may come to him. And, let your hair grow. Begin to look the way God wants you to look. Begin to act the way God wants to you act. I promise you, you will put a glorious shelter over him. God will anoint you to pray for him like you have never prayed for him before! Adam's Covering!

CHAPTER VI

SUMMARY

"And the Lord God said, it is not good that the man should be alone; I will make him a help meet for him" (Genesis 2:18).

Adam was alone. God said it was not good for him to be unaccompanied. Have you ever felt lonely? I mean alone both physically and emotionally. What a helpless feeling. Have you ever felt incomplete, like something was missing in your life?

God made a helpmeet for Adam from his own body. God took a rib and created a woman for him. God created Eve to make Adam complete as the two would be one flesh.

She was bone of his bone and flesh of his flesh. He went into a deep sleep. When he awoke, woman was there. She was to be a help or aid to him in life. She was to be his counterpart or mate, an extension of Adam's body. Adam called her woman or wife.

Adam was no longer alone. How about it? Can you remember the time you were so alone and then there came a friend or family member? How did you feel? It is not good for man to be by himself. There is an uncovered feeling when you are isolated. The woman was created for the man, not for him to abuse but to cherish.

She is to be the man's glory, his splendor, dignity, reputation and honor.

"For a man indeed ought not cover his head, forasmuch as he is the image and glory of God: but the woman is the glory of the man" (I Corinthians 11:7).

Adam could not change his condition of being alone, only God could by creating a woman. Man was not to cover his head by his own power for that would dishonor his head or Christ.

Yet the woman if uncovered dishonoureth her head or man, seeing she is his glory.

Adam is the glory, the splendor, dignity, reputation and honor of God. Eve is the glory of Adam. The woman is very important in the covering of the man just as the cherubims were in covering the Glory of God above the mercy seat.

Adam was alone or uncovered. God brought to him, from Adam's own flesh, a covering in a helpmeet called woman.

"But if a woman have long hair, it is a glory to her: for her hair is given her for a covering" (I Corinthians 11:15). Notice it reads to her not for her.

In her covering, there lies the glory of man. His dignity and reputation are held in the covering of woman.

"Every man praying or prophesying, having his head covered, dishonoureth his head. But every woman that prayeth or prophesieth with her head uncovered, dishonoureth <u>her head</u>: for that is even all one as if she were shaven" (I Corinthians 11:4-5).

If the head of a man is covered by his own power then he dishonoureth his <u>head or Christ</u>. If the woman is uncovered then she dishonoureth her <u>head or man</u>. "But I would have you to know, that the <u>head</u> of every man is Christ; and the <u>head</u> of the woman is the man; and the head of Christ is God" (I Corinthians 11:3).

We have already read where the woman's hair was given to her for a covering. The cherubims covered God's glory with their feathers as does the uncut hair of a woman cover the glory of man.

"For the man is not of the woman; but the woman of the man. Neither was the man created for the woman; but the woman for the man. <u>For this cause</u> ought the woman to have power on her <u>head</u> because of the angels"

(I Corinthians 11:8-10).

This is a comparison between the cherubim and women covering the glory of God and man. Could this power refer to the covering of her head or man? Yes, I believe it does. God gave her the influence of covering the man.

So many times men look down on women. Often, men think they do not need women. They credit themselves as being able to handle everything on their own. When men exclude women, they become uncovered and alone, open to the attacks of the enemy. Their honor becomes tarnished.

Men do not want to think of a woman being his

character but the Bible says not to be contentious for there is no other custom then this (I Corinthians 11:16).

If a man commits sin most of the time the woman stands fast in God. Her reputation is really not questioned when the man sins. The Church seems to fight through and in many cases spiritually grow because the women are standing, praying, and holding onto God.

But if a wife sins the reputation and honor of the man is often under question. He has a far harder time holding on to God and it seems the Church is now open to the various attacks of the enemy. Look at the many examples and I feel you will find this true in most of the cases.

Women have the power to cover their husband, their homes, and the Church from the attacks of the enemy.

When women cut their hair and begin to live a life not in line with biblical teaching, especially for those in leadership positions, havoc presses into the lives of their husbands, families and their Church. They uncovered their head. This opens them to all kinds of attacks.

Sure even if the woman is living a life pleasing to God her husband can sin, but when he is covered, it is harder for the enemy to destroy him. I am not blaming the woman for a spouse that chooses to sin.

I hope *Adam's Covering* has blessed your heart and has shed light on the importance of women in the body of Christ!

ISBN 141203312-8